Katty &
Two ok
spirits
love
Dennis Shiver

True Stories

to

Read Aloud

True Stories to Read Aloud

Dennis Shives

Meadow Dancer Press

Ojai, California

True Stories to Read Aloud

Copyright © 2014 Dennis E. Shives

All rights reserved

Published and distributed by:
Meadow Dancer Press
P. O. Box 1162
Ojai, CA 93024
dennisshivesojai@gmail.com
https://www.facebook.com/pages/Dennis-Shives-Artist/263894860420006

Contact us for information on author interviews or speaking engagements.

First Edition

Printed in the United States of America

Edited by Sonia Nordenson

Printed by CreateSpace, an Amazon.com company

Available on Kindle and other devices

ISBN-13: 978-1503083035

ISBN-10: 1503083039

In memory of Hugh Estill, who provided me with

the physical and psychological space to create.

Contents

Preface

I write these stories to remind myself of the magic all around me. Each one proves to be a good way to slow down and be in the moment with the events that have shaped my life. While some were profound moments of real learning, it took years for me to realize the wisdom in some of the others. All of the stories are true.

To me, life is very much like a walk in the woods. It's not how far I go, but how deep. It's easy to run through life, in order to get away from fear and adversity. But to slow down, to stop for as long as it takes to look, and listen, and try to understand something new, takes real bravery.

It was taking the time to learn how to draw and paint in color that helped me overcome my childhood fears. I have worked with music, singing and playing in front of large audiences. I've worked at float building, sand sculpting, and the invention of toys. Making masks and carving totem poles helps me to feel a kinship to the ancient stewards of this beautiful land.

My mother and grandmother were both so helpful to me. Countless other people inspired me to continue my study of natural things. I should thank them all. Thanks, Grandpa.

Following my creative spirit has brought me many surprises. I do a much better job at things when my heart is in them. It's with a grateful heart that I bring these simple stories to you. My purpose is to shine my little light, maybe entertain you for a moment in this vast universe, and then set you free.

Dennis Shives
Ojai, California
December 2014

Acknowledgments

My thanks to Sonia Nordenson for her excellent editing and sensitivity to my voice.

And, to my friend and life partner, Laurie Edgcomb, I give not just my warmest thanks but also my heart.

Fledged

Up a local canyon not far from home, there's a small pool at the base of a waterfall where I like to cool off on hot days. It's a couple of miles uphill, and well off the beaten trail. After many years of visiting this spot, I've found that the animals have become accustomed to my daily passings.

Early one spring, the creek was flowing cold and deep. On a rock face at the back of the pool, there's a narrow crack about five feet above the water line. Over the last few weeks, I'd noticed some grass sticking out, and I suspected it to be a bird's nest. When I came to swim, I tried not to look at it for fear of scaring the birds. I could imagine a little canyon wren, hunkered down and watching me.

I probably should have found another place to cool off, but this was the only pool deep enough to get wet in. Being rather good at justifying things in my own favor, I decided my presence was helping to protect the nest. The mother wren did seem to get used to my comings and goings.

On this particular day, I'd forgotten all about the birds and was standing lost in dreaming when suddenly something soft and fluffy landed on my head. At first I thought it was a bat, and I fought the urge to slap it off. Then I felt its little feet clinging to my hair.

I put the picture together in my mind: it had to be a baby bird from the nest. On its first attempt at flight, it must have been kind of frightened. The wings flapped as it tried to find its balance, and then it sat still. I could feel its warmth, and its weight shifting back and forth as it turned its head to observe the surroundings from its new perch.

I stood very still, feeling honored to have been chosen as a landing site. After a little while, the new aeronaut pulled itself together enough to risk another flight. Gathering all its courage and strength, it stood up, flapped those wonderful tiny wings, and lifted off.

As my fledgling friend headed up the creek, I caught sight of the proud parents, who were flying alongside with chirps of encouragement. I settled back into the water, reached up to smooth my hair, and found a little gift from the baby wren.

Flash Flood

It was a big winter storm in California, a maritime polar with a tropical fetch that brought warm, heavy rain for many days in a row. I was young and new to the world, so it was a scary and uncertain time in my life. My older brother, Bob, loved adventure, and often took me along to teach me about the wonders of nature.

One night, when the rain finally stopped, we could hear a distant roar coming from the direction of our small creek. I remember it being late and a very dark, moonless night. My brother got his flashlight and we headed off toward the roar.

When we got there, the sound was unbelievable. The ground shook from the force of the water as it rolled huge boulders downstream. Our creek had turned into a mighty torrent, washing away several rows of lemon trees as it carved a new channel down the valley.

We got close to the water, and noticed flashes of light coming from deep in the muddy turbulence. We turned off the flashlight, and as our eyes got used to the darkness, the flashes became much brighter. (I remember thinking about those flood flashes much later in life when I saw lightning bugs for the first time.)

The water was so much like chocolate milk that we couldn't tell what was making all the lights. My brother said, "I think it's the rocks bumping together underwater—causing sparks."

I remember watching the whole river blinking on and off with tiny bursts of light as far as we could see, and thinking, *Maybe that's why they call it a flash flood.*

Barbecue 90210

Tom Weddle and I got a job in Beverly Hills. Barbara was going to open a women's shoe store, and she needed a little help with the interior woodwork.

It was a good thing we didn't have any experience working downtown. There are more things you can't do than you can do, down there. The only day we could deliver materials was on Sunday, because there was no place to park. On Sunday the lane by the curb was closed to traffic. The lumberyard was about ten blocks away, but it took two hours to get there and back. No wood could be used on the outside of the building. Everything needed a permit. Permits had to go before the City Council, and the next meeting was in two weeks.

Lucky for us, Barbara was beautiful. She could go to the city and come back with permits that they'd told me would take three months. I think if she stood by the tracks they would have stopped the train to see if she needed a ride.

Tom and I arrived every Sunday night to unload materials, and we slept in the store all week. In Beverly Hills, everything was about twice as expensive as anywhere else, including food. I remember buying a twenty-two-dollar ham sandwich with a three-dollar soda pop (this was in 1974).

One Thursday we were tired of eating out. We decided to get a couple of New York steaks, French bread, beans, and potato salad and have us a barbecue in the alley. We took a trash can lid, filled it up with briquettes, and made a grill out of clothes hangers. We put the lid upside down on the metal trashcan and lit it up out in the alley just off Bedford Drive.

We got the bread and beans done first, and had started cooking the meat when we heard the first siren. Tom said, "That sounds like a fire truck. I wonder what's burning."

About ten seconds later, both ends of the alley were darkened by huge red machines. The firemen jumped off the trucks and ran toward us with hoses, fire axes, and extinguishers. They came up to our little barbecue just as I was taking off the last steak.

Someone who sounded like a fire captain said, "You can't do this in Beverly Hills."

They put out our briquettes. After they explained the rules to us, we said we were sorry, went back into our half-built shoe store, and had a cold steak dinner.

I see now why everybody eats out in Beverly Hills instead of having a barbecue.

Louie's Outing

The night was a foggy one, there on the beach at San Simeon. The clouds were backlit by a full moon. It was August 5, 1998, and I had driven north to get out of the hundred-degree weather in Ojai. I parked by a chain-link fence, under eucalyptus trees hanging over the road. The field next to me, with thirty or forty big Black Angus inside, I knew to be locally called "the Bullpen." I went to sleep early after my long drive.

I woke up about midnight to strange sounds. The bulls had moved down close to me. I heard a scraping sound, and opened a door to see what was going on. As my eyes adjusted to the light of the moon, I saw a bull rubbing on the fence, stretching it out. I could hear the tie wires popping off and whirling away. The chain-link fence that had been ten feet away when I went to bed was now scraping against the side of my van.

The fence shuddered as the bull rubbed along it. Then he turned his head and picked up the whole fence with his right ear. Now I was wide-awake! The bull, which I nicknamed "Louie," started pushing under the fence. Just as it looked like he would make a clean break, he stopped and started moving back and forth, scratching a hard-to-get place apparently long neglected.

After a minute that seemed like an hour, my bull Louie slipped under the fence, walked across the road, and began to graze. Then more bulls, moving through the dry leaves, breaking branches, came and gathered by the fence. They were looking at Louie, butting each other, and making sounds. I would describe their speech as perhaps similar to that of whales out of water. It started as a low-pitched rumble and very quickly jumped to a high-pitched blare that loosened the wax in my ears.

As I sat watching, a second bull picked up the fence in the exact same place that Louie had. With no effort whatsoever, he put his ear under, gave a little lift, and walked casually out onto the road. Then, as though he'd forgotten something, or remembered something, he turned and moseyed back over to the fence, stuck his ear down, picked up the fence again, and ducked back into the bullpen, never to come out again. I have no idea why I do some things, so I didn't even try to figure out what he was thinking.

Old Louie stayed out all night, munching grass. It was a restful sound. No one flying down the road going seventy would have liked to know what I knew. But there was no one to tell anyway, so I went back to bed.

In the morning, a cowboy in a pickup truck came by slapping a rope on the outside of his door. He walked Louie to an open gate up the road a ways, and back in Louie went.

Some ranch workers put barbed wire on the back of the chain link fence that same day.

If, perchance, you come up behind an old VW van going kind of slow, some foggy night, it's just me—thinking about that big black bull standing in the road, grazing.

The Coming of the King

Dunning's Lagoon was finally quiet. It was my first spring in Alaska, where I had come to build a house. The oil spill had just happened, and the old LCM6 Navy landing craft had been hired to haul a big Anapol tank. (Anapol was a detergent used to cause the oil to sink from the water's surface and to wash the beach in Prince William Sound.)

Every able-bodied man, woman, or kid around had been scooped up and employed for the summer, so they were all gone. The salmon season had just opened, and I was glad to be alone. I had a small cabin to sleep in, a wooden skiff named Beefy (locally made by Dave Seaman), a large bag of money to buy whatever I needed, and free rein on the design of the house at hand.

Everything was new to me. As my client, Jack, had left, he'd said, "You're on your own. I'll be back in September." It seemed like I had just won the lottery—maybe better.

My first few days were spent drawing, making lists, and running back and forth to Homer, fifteen miles away, to get materials. After a while I settled in to a rhythm of working.

Up on the roof one morning, I was putting in rafters when up above me the resident eagle let out a big scream. I looked up to see what was going on. The eagle was looking down the inlet toward a strange disturbance in the water. The tide was low, but coming in. There on the surface was a bumping, swirling, splashing shape maybe fifty feet wide and three hundred feet long. It swung back and forth like a huge sea monster.

I stood up and watched it come. I remember thinking no one was going to believe this one. Just as it couldn't get any more thrilling, the eagle screamed again, and with his talons hanging down he jumped into a slow glide toward the monster. It was about then that I realized the monster was a school of large salmon, and I was going to get my first look at an eagle catching a fish.

The bird swooped down close to the water and grabbed something. Then suddenly he was gone. Somehow I didn't think it would go like that. After what seemed like minutes, a white head popped up and then went down again. By then the eagle's mate had flown up and was circling around overhead, screaming.

The white head came up again, and the eagle began to swim with his wings toward shore. It wasn't pretty; the fish was still very much alive, and was dragging the bird around at will. Straining and fighting, the eagle had locked in his talons and couldn't have let go if he wanted to.

Swimming with waterlogged wings, the great bird of prey finally dragged the fish up onto the beach, and his mate came down to help. Together they dismantled that king salmon. The eagle, at about twenty pounds, had landed a fish of at least twenty-five pounds. I was impressed. I climbed down and went and made myself a hot chocolate.

A note of explanation: As schools of salmon move into shallow water, the fish on the top are pushed out of the water by those underneath, giving, from a distance, the appearance of a huge, shiny monster splashing and squirming along. This might be where some sea monster stories come from.

Into the Storm

From year to year, Alaskan summers are never the same. The far north has a whole different idea of how to celebrate the return of the sun each year. It's sometimes surprisingly soft and gentle, but hardly ever.

It was light outside, and the Steller's jays were playing on the round front porch. I woke up when I heard the first mild gust of wind. I knew from experience that when the breeze came from that direction, the northwest, we were in for a blow.

It was one of many storms that season. First the wind came, slowly building to sixty, seventy, even eighty MPH, in huge gusts that would relax for a few minutes and then start over again. Although I needed food, and materials for the house I was building, it was a fearful time to go to town. I remember giving myself permission to take the day off.

As I sat hunkered down upstairs, drinking coffee by the seven-foot round window, I could see whitecaps out in the channel. I heard a boat start up around the corner, and down the lagoon came a little yellow sixteen-foot wooden skiff. It was Barbara Seaman, all bundled up in rain gear and looking more like an astronaut then a sailor. With her in the front sat three-year-old Nate and five-year-old Alder, in full rain gear, laughing and singing.

Barbara was standing up, with the outboard motor steering handle between her legs. One hand was blocking the wind, and the other firmly grasping the throttle, with the red ripcord tied to her glove-covered hand. (The ripcord will kill the motor if you fall out of the boat, so that it doesn't keep going without you.) She was headed for Homer with her kids.

Barbara's husband, Dave, was employed for the summer using their fishing boat as a salmon tender. Barbara was the mail lady, and it was Thursday. She and the kids were going in to pick up the mail for Dunning's Laguna. It was fifteen miles to town—two hours in a skiff on a nice day. More than half the trip was across the open ocean.

A heavy rain began to fall. I looked down at my own reflection on the surface of my coffee and pondered the big sissy looking back at me. As I looked back up, I saw a very brave woman, heading off into the storm with her two most precious "possessions."

I got bundled up in layers, grabbed my lists, loaded the skiff, and headed off to Homer.

Bubble Bears

After delivering a propane truck for winter fuel to the native people on Illumina Lake, we pulled out of Kamishak Bay into a full-blown storm coming down the Cook Inlet. The waves were twenty feet high and it was blowing about forty knots.

As the waves hit the loading gate on the front of our LCM6 landing craft, the grating on top cut everything into neat squares of green water that looked like flying bales of hay. They were arching to the back of the boat and hitting the windshield, making it very hard to see. The well deck was filling up faster than the bilge could drain it, so Captain Jack Estill decided it was time to swing into the next little bay and wait out the blow.

Soon we were in calm water behind a hill. We dropped the hook, and as we settled down and made dinner I saw that the beach was full of brown bears feeding on salmon in a big creek at the head of the bay.

After watching for a while, I noticed that the wind was blowing onshore, and decided to see what the bears thought about bubbles. I got out my trusty bubble brush and sent a steady stream of joyfully bouncing bubbles across the water toward the shore.

The bears began to notice the bubbles coming at them, and each one had a different reaction. Some stood up and batted at them, some bit and snapped at them, and one great big male took off at a dead run up and over the beach bluff. He kept going over the second hill behind; it was very entertaining.

The bears returned the favor later on that evening. We had dinner, then settled down and went to sleep. When I woke up, I noticed that the boat was no longer rocking. The tide had gone out, and the boat was sitting on the sandy bottom. I got up to see where an odd scratching noise was coming from. Sliding open the plywood back door, I stepped out on the mezzanine behind the steering house.

From where I stood, all I could see at first were three big sets of bear tracks in the sand leading down to the boat. The deck was about eight feet off the sand. Mother brown bear and two cubs were busy chewing barnacles off the side of the landing craft. When they heard the door open, they all stood up to look. The mother bear's paws easily reached the back deck. I jumped back in the deckhouse and slammed the door behind me.

Everyone else on board had slept through the whole thing, so I went back to bed. When I awoke again, we were afloat. We started the engines and headed for home.

Riders on the Storm

Summer's end is a powerful time for all life in Alaska. During the long days of never-ending daylight, everyone knows what's coming.

I can feel the change. The light starts to shorten. Then, one night in mid-August, it gets dark, and stars can be seen for the first time in months. The blueberries are ripe. The fireweed blooms all the way to the top, and there is a slight chill in the morning air. The squirrels are busy gathering food for winter. The silver salmon run is over, and waves start to break on the Homer spit after being absent all summer.

The high tides of August's full moon are the biggest of the year—twenty-two feet in and out every twelve hours. For one hour, the bottom of the lagoon is completely exposed.

In order to leave, I have to wait for the water to return. I look around for my airline ticket and check the date of departure against the calendar. One week to go. Then it gets cold. Half asleep one night, I wander outside to the outhouse, where it feels like I'm peeing in the refrigerator.

The next day, all the leaves fall off the blueberry bushes, leaving only the fruit. More bears come around. Then the native women come, with their children, to pick blueberries. The woods are alive with talk and laughter as they strip the forest clean. Everyone has blue hands and faces.

Finally the birds begin to gather in huge numbers—many different kinds of ducks and geese. The sandhill cranes are circling the bay, calling out to the family. Day after day the flocks get bigger, and then, on the day before I leave, the wind begins to blow. A big winter storm is coming in, and all the birds begin to rise, almost in unison.

By the next day the skies are covered with migrating birds; they nearly block out the sun, and the sound is deafening. They are riding each other's wing wake. My flight is leaving at eight that night. I close down the house, load the boat, and make a pass around the lagoon like the birds, saying goodbye.

As I cross Kachemak Bay, the sun is going down. A huge wall of clouds closes in from the northwest. Wave after wave of mallards, sandpipers, storm petrels, Canadian honkers, tundra swans, and sandhill cranes fill the red evening sky.

They're rising higher and higher into the leading edge of the storm, like surfers paddling to catch a huge wave. The only thing missing is Andrea Bocelli singing "Time to Say Goodbye."

As I check my bags and board my connector flight to Anchorage, I can hear the birds out in the darkness. We take off, up into the storm, and as we rise higher the ride gets really rough, finally smoothing out above the clouds. As we turn north toward Anchorage, we fly into the long colored curtains of the aurora borealis.

I never saw a summer end with such beauty and drama. Hallelujah!

Resurrection

I have a friend, "Grandpa," whose youngest daughter decided to become a nun. She gave away all of her stuff, went up to the cloister, and got accepted for a trial period.

After a few months, we received a letter from the head mother. It seemed the nuns' carved wooden corpus of Christ (beautifully made in Italy) was in need of cleaning and repair. Could we do it?

"Yes!" was the answer, of course. We picked it up out in front of the cloister and brought it home.

Grandpa sanded the form, cleaned it, and fixed one knee and a toe. He polished it, sealed it back up, and hid a little note in it for the next repairperson to read. Then it was time to take it back.

I had always wondered what it was like to be on the inside of a convent, and as fate would have it I was elected to help take Jesus back.

Jesus was big—I figured about six feet eight inches tall—and weighed in at one hundred sixty pounds. With his arms splayed out, he didn't fit in the bed of the pickup, so we had to tie him down in full sight of other drivers. This caused quite a stir as we started up the freeway.

People followed, honking, waving, and yelling out their windows. I couldn't help but think of the original crucifixion, on the way to Golgotha. We were a good hour on the road, and were amazed by all the different emotional reactions.

We finally pulled up to the nunnery and backed up to those big gates that very few pass through (somehow I thought they'd be pearly). It was a religious experience when those gates swung open and the whole courtyard was full of smiling, round-faced, sparkling-eyed nuns. There at the end of the rose garden stood a huge empty cross.

Grandpa got Jesus by the feet and I grabbed the neck. We wobbled down that pathway, just like in the story, and leaned him up against the cross. Now our task was to hang him back up.

Our first try was a failure. He was just too heavy for one person to hold while the other tightened the bolts from the back.

I went out and got the tie-down rope from the truck. We made a noose around his neck, ran the rope up over the top of the cross, and slowly pulled Jesus up. His form looked so real that it was an amazing thing to watch. Ever so gently we lined up the bolt holes, and finally screwed him back onto the cross.

The sound of clapping started out softly; all the nuns were crying. As we took the ladder down and moved back away from the cross, I noticed that the rose garden was in full bloom.

On the way back home, Grandpa didn't say much. About halfway back, we decided we'd better stop at Frostie's and have a big chocolate shake to calm our nerves.

When we eventually talked about it, we both felt like we'd been to the crucifixion and the resurrection on the same day.

Boody

Business has never been my strong point. When I make a deal with someone, I almost always wind up giving away something I made and owing something besides. But there was one exception to this long tradition of mine.

Beulah Robertson (or Boody, as she was known by all the people who loved her, and everybody did) needed a wooden sign made. Her sister's husband, Harold, was opening a custom meat-cutting store in Arizona. Boody didn't have a lot of money, so if I made the sign for Harold she said she'd be glad to trade me for some homemade pies. We worked out the price at so much a pie, and it came out to twenty-five pies.

Just to let you in on some history, Boody was famous for her pies. She knew how to make them from scratch, and she won the Ventura County Fair lemon meringue pie contest seven years in a row.

Boody's pies were legendary. I found them to be not easy to share. For years I would go out in the backcountry and pick wild berries and chokecherries for her to use in pies.

When I met her, Boody was in her eighties. One day I was sitting at her big round oak table when someone from the Madonna Inn called from San Louis Obispo to say, "We tasted some of your homemade jellies, and we'd like to use them exclusively in our Inn." Boody smiled and very humbly said, "I would love to help you, but I'm too old."

She'd bought her simple little home by selling twenty-five-cent hamburgers inside the old Bayless Market in Ojai. "*That* was a lot of hamburgers," she once remarked. She was a living treasure to all who had the honor of knowing her.

Now, working as an artist has never paid very well, and eating is a very important part of living. I would be slaving away, acting on some silly idea or another about a project my internal voice had directed me to make, and starving to death, when I'd hear an ever-so-soft tapping on the back door of my shop.

And a sweet little voice would say, "It's Boody. I have a pie for you . . ."

Bull Tails

I have some strange connection to bulls. I remember how, back when I was very young, we visited the Black Hills one summer. I got out of the car to see buffalo up close behind the fence. One huge bull walked over, looked me right in the eye, threw his head back, and let out a buffalo bellow so loud my heart stopped for a moment. I took off running, dove into the car, and climbed up in the back window and hid.

I've been hooked ever since. Whenever I get a chance to hang out and watch bulls, I do. Here are some stories from my observations.

The late, great Bob Donlan used to run cattle on the old Bar-M Ranch of five thousand acres, up east of Los Alamos. Once, while visiting the ranch, I sat and watched a particularly handsome big red bull standing by a fence. One by one the cows would graze their way down the fence line, and each would wind up stopping with her tail directly under Big Red's nose. He would take a deep breath and hold his head up high and show some teeth. He appeared to be grinning. This routine went on all afternoon.

On another day, two bulls got to fighting. They were pretty serious. Pushing and shoving, they broke through a barbed wire fence and out onto the freeway, causing a major traffic jam. Bob had a big stud horse that he threw a saddle on, and he grabbed his pistol, some birdshot, and a rope.

Out onto the freeway he rode, shouting and shooting, trying to stop the battle. Nothing seemed to work, until one bull saw Bob's horse and started chasing it. Bob rode back through the hole in the fence, and the two bulls followed him. He made it look so easy. As we fixed the fence, happy people drove by honking.

Another time, further up the coast, I was walking down a quiet beach. As I came around a corner, there were bulls down on the sand: three Black Angus and the biggest elephant seal I had ever seen. I didn't have a camera with me, so I later painted a picture of the scene. The bulls were standing there, all around the elephant seal, with their tails sticking out in disbelief.

The seal had his head up in the air, fully extended. He was about eight feet high from his front flippers to the top of his nose, and at least that much more of him lay on the ground. All three of the two-thousand-pound Angus bulls would have easily fit inside his hide. He was making those deep rattling sounds that you can hear for miles. What made the scene even more interesting was the square radar-tracking box attached to the elephant seal's head. It looked like a hat.

It appeared to me that the bulls were amazed at how big that seal was. I know I was. They stood around him for a while longer, and then moseyed off to graze.

Yet another time, I arrived at the ranch and got to the bullpen just in time to see some bulls arrive in a trailer. I'm not sure if they were new bulls or being brought back from the cows, but they were in an uproar. There were bulls in the field and some in the trailer, and all the bulls were bellowing. The old bulls stayed way back, but made the most noise. The younger bulls came running down acting real tough. They stood around the tailgate waiting for the new guys to come out.

All of a sudden, out came a smaller red bull. He put his head down and charged, catching the nearest big Black Angus in mid-bellow. He banged into him and nearly knocked him down. The red bull charged again, and chased the bigger bull up and over the hill. The other young bulls moved back, and all the new bulls climbed out and started to graze. The big old bulls never joined the fray. They just stood way back, bellowing. I couldn't help but laugh at the similarities to human behavior. They're just like us.

I was out early one morning in a place I call the Magic Forest. The moss- and lichen-covered oak trees there all lean over; the wind has bent them. They grow in extreme adversity, reminding me of the human soul. The whole forest stands about fifteen feet tall. The trees are full grown—some sixty feet long—but they lie on their side.

I pushed through the spring grass that had just started to grow, keeping a sharp eye out because the bulls use this place to nap when the wind starts to blow and they're hard to see in the shade.

Then, off in the trees, I spotted something black. As I cautiously approached the black thing, it turned into a hairy knot tied around a limb about waist-high. It was the swishy end of a bull's tail. It looked like the bull had flicked his tail at some flies, hit a limb in doing so and wrapped the tail around it, and got himself caught. He must have given it a tug and thought something had him, panicked, and taken off—leaving his fly swatter behind.

I saved the bull tail to remind myself not to jump to conclusions when I feel threatened. I never did find the bull . . . I wonder how far he ran.

Giving Back

It was high summer in Montana on the Red Rock Lakes—my first visit to the area. I'd hauled up some furniture from California for a new log cabin in the Centennial Valley (near Odell Creek, at the foot of Little Sheep Mountain). I stayed on a couple of weeks to restore an old Basque sheepherder's wagon—a guesthouse for future visitors to the ranch.

At that time of year, rivulets of melted snow run through the flat pasturelands, full of spawning Arctic grayling. Yellowstone National Park is two hours away from there, down a dirt road due east. To me, everything was new. There were plenty of beaver dams, and buffalo, moose, and deer were everywhere. There were also bighorn sheep on the mountain to the south.

I think my favorite animal, though, was the pronghorn antelope. They liked to be out in the open so they could see what was coming. We would race them down the road with our truck while they ran along beside us on the other side of the fence. Once, while racing them at fifty miles an hour, we hit a small creek. The water went over the top of the truck; it took an hour to dry off the electrical system and get the truck started again. That was our last race.

Another day my friend Jerry and I went way down the valley to an area we hadn't seen before. It was bottomland, the kind antelope like. Way off, out in the dried-out pasture, I saw a little green patch in the middle of the field. There were several antelope standing around there, eating the grass. It caught my eye.

I said, "Stop—I want to take a closer look at that green patch."

I climbed out of the truck and went to see. As I got nearer, I could see some bones sticking out of the grass. Lying there was a winterkill antelope. The seeds from its stomach had sprouted, and the nutrients from the meat had fertilized the ground all around it. The grass was two feet tall, and the other antelopes were grazing on it.

Finding that site was a wonderful gift to me. It was a lesson on giving back.

Varmint Call

I was climbing a familiar old trail that was muddy after a spring rain. Walking barefoot to feel the mud between my toes, I trudged quietly upward, headed for a campground called The Pines. My mind was wandering when I began to hear a strange, almost distressed, sound—that of a lost or injured animal, perhaps.

I was intrigued. Continuing uphill, I tried to imagine what sort of animal would make such a sound. As I got closer, the whimpering call was clearer, and it sounded like a large bird.

Finally I rounded the last corner of the trail, and began to search the treetops. Stepping quietly on dry pine needles, I moved toward the sound. Then I stopped in my tracks.

About thirty feet away, hanging down about head high from a tree branch, I saw the long, golden tail of a mountain lion. The cat continued to make the strange birdcall sounds.

He had lured me right in. I slowly backed down the trail, still hearing the catbird call. The lion had not seen me; it was looking uphill.

I have never heard this behavior described before. It seemed as if the lion had a varmint call, and I was the varmint. Well, this varmint got away!

Tick Talk

Up on a trail in the springtime, right after some rain, I felt an itch on the back of my knee. I stopped and scratched and found that a small black bug had dug a hole in my skin and started dining on me. How rude! I got hold of it and pulled it out.

It was tiny. I put on my glasses and took a closer look. It was a female American dog tick. She had a lovely white line around the shield on her back. She was hungry; probably wanted some blood so she could lay her eggs. They lay thirty thousand each, from what I hear. I didn't like this thought, especially after being bitten.

I took my new little blood sister (we shared the same blood now) and put her in a plastic tube that I carry for superglue. As I walked on down the trail, I began to notice more little ticks hanging out on the ends of the grass and twigs. The thought came to mind, *Gosh— they want to go with me.* I started picking them off the bushes and putting them in my little plastic tube.

Soon I had so many it was hard to keep them in when I caught a new one. I had to hit the tube on a rock, knocking them all to the bottom for long enough to drop the next one in.

When I got home, I thought, *What am I going to do with all these little monsters?* I was looking around when I saw the microwave sitting there.

I set it for one minute, and in they went, tube and all. It worked very well. They all stopped crawling. Then I dumped them in a plastic sandwich container and put the lid on.

It became a little ritual I did every day after that. I would come home from my hike with some ticks and put them in the microwave, where they would dance around for a few seconds and stop. Then into my collection they would go.

After a while it got harder to find them. I collected about four thousand ticks. *What do you do with that many ticks?* I asked my subconscious mind one night. The answer surprised even me: *Make a clock!* I got out the glue and the tweezers and went at it.

I first made a circle out of plastic, then used the ticks to make the numbers, and then drilled a hole and put an electric clock motor in. Then I glued ticks on the hands, too.

It's been a couple of years now since I made my clock. It's sort of gross to have a tick clock, but what else would you do with four thousand mean little bugs?

The trail has been pretty much tick-free ever since. When I look at my clock, I always think about how every other tick on it was female, and she didn't lay thirty thousand eggs to grow up and bite me—or anyone else. It's a comforting thought. Let's see, two thousand females times thirty thousand is sixty million eggs.

Tick Tock!

Ol' B.G.

I never could tell whether B.G. was a friend or a competing constituent, but I kind of liked him. Ol' B.G. was a wood-carver from Oklahoma. He made owls, eagles, dolphins, turtles, and mermaids out of wood. He'd get a piece of wood and sit and look at it for a while, then go to yanking the rope of his chainsaw and cussing because it wouldn't ever start. When it finally did, he'd start making cuts and shaping stuff, stopping every once in a while to roll a smoke. B.G. did okay on animals, but he had a hard time on people's faces.

He was most inspired when he had some place he wanted to go, like Fiji. One day he said he felt like travelling, so he set out to make a mermaid to sell to get the money to go.

He worked and worked and smoked and worked, but he was having a lot of trouble with the face of that mermaid. After several days, he got mad and sort of gave up. He got in his truck and took off.

Now, to this very day I don't know why I went over and started looking at that face while he was gone. Or why I decided to give him a hand.

I opened her eyes, gave her a cute little smile, fixed the nose, braided the hair, and made her look real nice. I felt proud of myself for being so helpful; I just knew he would like what I'd done.

Well, when I came back the next day, there was B.G., and he was mad as hell. He said something about who did I think I was, messing with his wood carving. I thought he was going to hit me. So I told him I was sorry, and swore I wouldn't help any more. Ol' B.G. finally cooled down a little bit, threw that mermaid in his pickup truck, and roared off.

I heard the next day that he sold that thing for twenty-five hundred dollars to the first person he showed it to, and I didn't see him again for six months. I still don't know what I learned about helping others from this experience . . . and he never did thank me!

Everyday Wonders

It was March, and I was once again visiting Cambria. Having slept up near Hearst Castle, I headed for town to get some coffee at Don's Coffee Roasting Company. The east wind had been blowing most of the night, so the beach was warm and clear.

I decided to sit outside. The sun was just cracking over the horizon, and the stereo was playing Bocelli in the background. As I sat sipping my coffee and beginning to wake up, the sky suddenly filled with turkey vultures, all taking to the air at once from the eucalyptus trees behind the building. The orange sunrise was lighting up the bottoms of their wings.

As they gathered in a huge flock (over a hundred) and began to circle to gain height, the music changed to the Hallelujah Chorus. The vultures climbed higher as Handel's oratorio reached more powerful levels, and as the music peaked the birds broke from their beautiful swirling dance and drifted off in all directions.

I sat there for a few minutes with my spirit hanging open, then looked around and realized that I was the only one who'd seen the vulture performance.

As I walked away, I noticed that the sparrows were eating bugs off the hoods of the parked cars. I thanked the dawn spirits for a wonder-filled morning.

Horsequake

Late one summer I was returning from digging for dinosaurs in North Dakota. The cold had me headed south. The trees were turning colors, and the geese were flying in big "V"s—my favorite time of year. I was driving down Highway 93 in eastern Nevada. No big hurry.

As the sun dropped low in the west, I started looking for a dirt side road. I like to camp off the main road a ways. I remember passing over a cattle guard and driving up over a hill, out of the sight and sound of the highway. I made myself a sandwich and went out and wandered around till it got too dark to see. As I fell asleep, I was still listening to the honkers.

In the morning I awoke to an earthquake. My van was shaking back and forth so violently that I sat up to see the devastation.

Out the back window, I saw a big hairy animal rubbing back and forth against the side of my coach. As it turned a little, I could see in the faint light the profile of a big white horse. Then more horses appeared, milling around and nipping and kicking each other. I guess I started laughing, because the shaking stopped as the animals moved away.

Later, as I headed back down toward the highway, I caught up with the wild horses again. This time they galloped down the road and out into the sage flats. The seven mares ran along, looking back at the stallion behind them covering their retreat. He moved back and forth, looking at my van.

I could see that there was great respect and love among this herd of wild Mustangs. But what a way to wake up alone in the wilderness!

The Coral-Pink Sand Lion

Kanab, Utah. I was off on an adventure. A friend wanted to go figure out where the big bucks hang out before hunting season. The reason didn't matter to me; I just like being out in the woods.

We stopped downtown and talked deer, water holes, and big antlers with the local big buck winner from last year. He pointed us south, down toward the Kaibab National Forest. I remember thinking, *He hunts north of town, down near the border with the coral-pink sand dunes.*

The first night we spent in a campground, making camp next to a guy with seven women and about sixteen children. They were doing the same thing we were: checking out the prospective hunting.

As the sun went down, I had my first encounter with nighthawks, the long-winged nocturnal hunters that feed on flying insects. They would climb a hundred feet in the air and then pitch into a steep dive. The sound they made was very much like the sound produced by sticking a feather out your car window when you're going about eighty. They'd come swooping down, catch a moth, and pull out just inches before they hit the ground. This went on till well after dark.

The next morning we decided to head west, down a little-used two-track dirt road. Using low-range four-wheel drive, we crept on and on over the soft sand. When we finally stopped for lunch, I noticed that the odometer said we'd gone twenty-four miles. I remember commenting on how that was about as far as I wanted to walk back: "Let's hope we don't break down or get stuck."

Around the next bend, the road petered out at the base of a box canyon where we could see a distant cave under an outcropping. "Let's go see what's up there," one or the other of us said.

The gentle slope that led up the cliff was covered with pinyon pines, thick-trunked cedars, and creosote bush. As we climbed, I noticed some deer antlers in the shade. I pushed back a branch and found a complete skeleton, but didn't think much of it at the time. Up we climbed. Nearer to the cave entrance, more bones. The opening was larger then I'd thought, maybe thirty feet wide and ten feet tall. Going in, about sixty feet wide.

We noticed a squirrel tail and some small animal bones littered around an old coyote skull that appeared to have been gnawed on. All over the sandy floor of the cave were large mountain lion tracks, some quite fresh.

As we walked back out, I was looking at the view when I noticed all the deer skeletons—one and sometimes two under every tree in sight. From where I stood, I could count forty-four of them.

We stopped there, dazed by the sight before us. The spell was suddenly broken as over the top of our cave, about fifty feet above the summit, came an old camo-painted B-52, so close that the pilot waved to us as he disappeared over the next ridge. He must have been flying under the radar.

I remember looking back down at the boneyard below and seeing something shiny reflecting up at me. I climbed down the hill, keeping an eye on where it lay. There, under a stubby cedar tree, I found the source of the sparkle: a stainless steel arrowhead stuck in the shoulder socket of the front leg bone of a deer. I was fascinated; I cut the socket loose and stuck it in my pocket. We wandered around looking for about an hour, and came to the conclusion that we weren't the only deer hunters to have discovered this place.

Much later, when I found the bone piece in my jacket, I took it to a bone specialist doctor friend of mine to see what he thought of it. He said the broken leg had healed from the wound. The growth of the bone looked like about six months' worth before the lion caught the deer, and every movement must have been painful.

Later on, the thought would sometimes come to my mind, *Count your blessings, Dennis—things aren't so bad. You could have been that deer.* I keep that bone on my desk to remind myself.

Pipe Dream

The desert doesn't cost much to visit. Some gas, food, and a little time are all you need. I was getting away all alone this time, mostly because no one else had time to come with me. I tuned up the old VW van that's had me for thirty-eight years, grabbed the bare necessities, and took off. I stopped in Palm Springs to say hi to Denny Miller (the ex-Tarzan who used to live in Ojai), and then headed out into the Arizona unknown, ending up somewhere down Highway 8 near Gila Bend.

It was late February or early March, and the wildflowers were really good that year. I stopped a lot on the dirt road I'd chosen to explore, and finally parked down near the Gila River under the dappled cottonwood trees.

There was an irrigation canal coming from the side of a dam, set up to water some cotton fields. I was drawn to the slow-moving water in the ditch and, walking along, I saw that there were catfish—lots of catfish. From where I stopped, I could see hundreds of them, moving slowly around in a concrete canal too narrow to skip a stone in.

I walked a little farther and stopped on a single-lane bridge over the water to watch the action. All the fish were moving downstream, all together like one fish. I looked down at the bridge I was standing on. Under the road, a pipe as wide as a manhole opened into the canal. From the pipe, I could see something emerge. Something big.

A grey, thuggish kind of thing, almost as big as the pipe, was sticking out of the hole, and then moving out a little further. As the eyes came out and it saw me, it moved ever so slowly back into the darkness of the pipe, its long whiskers still visible.

It was the biggest freshwater fish I've ever seen—a six-foot-long channel cat, doing quite well out in the middle of the Sonoran Desert. I thanked the desert spirits for showing me such a magnificent old beast. It reminded me of the old saying "Bloom where you're planted."

The Meadow Dancer

A glorious spring bloom expected in the Temblor Range had me up in the highlands. It was indeed the most beautiful bloom I'd seen in many years. The hillsides were painted orange, purple, yellow, red, blue, and pink with wildflowers . . . a hundred thousand acres of fluorescent poppies splattered intermittently with lupine, daisies, hairy vetch, owl's clover, coast goldfields, and me.

I had pulled off the road at a wide spot near the top of a hill. Birds singing, bees buzzing, the aroma of flowers . . . it was dawn, and I was in heaven, with nothing but natural beauty for miles in every direction.

I had felt called to this place somehow. As I stood there soaking it all in, I began to hear a distant sound—far away at first, then closer: the labor of a small car climbing a steep grade. It sounded old and overloaded, downshifting as it climbed toward me in my private retreat. It was coming from the direction I was headed.

I thought, *That car is hauling someone who's going to disturb my peace here this morning, you just watch.* Slowly up the hill it labored, then it finally came around the corner and into view. And, sure enough, it began to slow down. I eased around behind my van, hoping to not be seen. The old Volvo turned in and pulled right up to where I was hiding. The driver's window rolled down, and a friendly voice from a kind face said, "Hi! I'm lost. Is this the way to Los Angeles?"

As I got over myself, I said, "Well sort of, but it's the long way around. It's a slow, curvy road for the next sixty miles. Where are you coming from?"

"San Francisco," was his reply. "I've been dancing there. I'm with the New York City Ballet. I have a show in L.A. tomorrow, and thought I'd take the scenic route down there. I've never seen so many wildflowers!"

Well, after that I sort of liked the guy, and we had us a good little chat. He was in his mid-twenties—healthy, happy, kind, and gentle—a great guy with a good heart. After a while he asked what I did and what I was doing out here in the middle of nowhere.

"I'm a self-taught lifelong artist and maker of silly toys. I love to see Mother Nature put on her Sunday best. I'm out smelling flowers and feeling thankful for being alive."

Since he'd said he was a dancer, I got to thinking he might like to see something fun, so I pulled out a couple of toys. I blew up a storm of beautiful bubbles of all sizes with my bubble brush, sending them drifting off in the soft morning breeze. Then I got out my latest thing: a wind-powered music box that plays "Greensleeves" as you swing it around. It's a pinwheel hooked to a music box mechanism that's mounted in a small megaphone.

I showed him how it worked, then handed it to him to try. He waved it around and made it go. And then, as if by magic, he whirled away, making music and spinning through the air. When he leaped, he seemed to just hang in midair forever, flying and landing like an antelope in one joyous bound after another. He danced—or flew— through the flower fields and across the road and back.

I was stunned by the young man's skill. He was magnificent, playing my music maker and dancing to the tune. His dance moves were the greatest I'd ever seen. On that remote country road at dawn, dancing to the sound of a wind-powered music box, he was a marvel.

Finally tiring, he walked over, gave the toy back to me, and said, "If you ever make more of those, I want a box full of them." Then he got back in his car, started it up, and was gone like a daydream.

I stood there for a long time, reflecting on what I'd just seen. Then came the thought, *I should call my new toy a Meadow Dancer, in honor of the man who flew.*

I hope he reads this story and gives me a call. It'd be nice for us to catch up.

An Anasazi Mother

The deserts of the Southwest . . . hot and dry, with cacti, rattlesnakes, Indians, and wild burros. They make a great place to visit in the spring and fall, especially after prolonged periods spent in the far north.

On a sea of heat and thirst, I like to float my mind across the idea of the desert. When I get there, I take off my shoes and let the sun dry up the moss between my toes. I build small fires in the evening and wander in the moonlight, getting used to the stillness.

As I walked one time, I came across a pile of pottery shards and imagined how someone must have slipped and dropped a pot full of precious water, coming back from the river fifteen hundred years ago. The pot was painted with beautiful and meaningful designs. I could see a bird and a symbol for rain, lying there in the rubble.

I dropped down closer to the Gila River. There were mounds of soft sand, far back away from the water. They appeared to be old adobe house ruins. As I stepped on the silty earth, I could see chipped stones here and there, from someone making arrowheads or scraper tools. Still more potshards; someone lived here for a long time. As I continued toward the river, I noticed I was being bitten by small flies and thought that must be why the houses were set so far back from the water.

Across the canyon, I could see stacked rocks up on top of a stone outcropping. It looked like a fort—some sort of defendable position. It occurred to me that it must not have been as peaceful there as I'd have liked to think. As I crossed the river, stepped up on two stones, and jumped to the far shore, I sank to my thighs in quicksand. Only then did I notice that the water smelled like sewage and laundry soap, and I struggled out of the mud remembering that Phoenix was only sixty miles upstream.

I climbed up the far bank through some creosote bush and made it to the bottom of the stone outcropping below the fort, where I began to see small chips pecked into the sunbaked black basalt cliffs. They were very old. They formed images of hunting scenes, desert bighorns fighting, circular spirals, and broad-shouldered shamans with horned hats. One amazing pecking showed ten warriors or hunters chasing sheep.

As I walked down the wall, and then around the end till I was out of sight of the rest of the ancient art, I noticed a smaller image—a stick figure. It was pecked very low to the ground, but with great care, and depicted a woman giving birth.

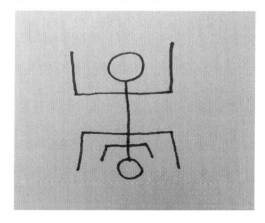

The Song Gate

I remember the first time I heard the song. It was early morning. I left the pavement behind and noticed the change of texture with the dirt road now under my bare feet. As I plodded along, the dust made a cloud with each step. Spring had found the chaparral, and the fragrance of the wildflowers was enhanced by the sweet smell of orange blossoms drifting up from orchards farther down the valley.

Across the pasture, three pack burros eyed me warily as I passed. Remembering some of the burdens I had carried, I felt a sort of kinship with them.

The gate really isn't much to look at, just a rusty green thing. It's hanging on a torch-cut piece of old drill pipe cemented in the ground fifty years ago, with barbed wire heading off in both directions from the posts.

As I unsnapped the chain, I became aware of just how peaceful that place is. It's so quiet that I could hear a valley quail chucking the alarm: There's a human coming! There's a human coming!

Along the trail, a few bees were hovering over their hives, now and than giving me a fly-by. The wind was pushing through the oak trees, and I could hear water softly splashing down a small seasonal creek nearby.

I gripped the gate and gently pulled it open, and it began to sing . . . The song started with a long, slow note, sounding like the bass string on a fine old cello being soulfully caressed by a well-resined horsehair bow. Then it jumped to high C, like an old blues man singing "Crossroads." The last sound was the three-note moan of a train whistle, out on a prairie somewhere far away.

I stood there for a moment, relishing the feelings the song had evoked. As I drifted back to the present, I became aware of what an important place I was standing in. This side of the song gate was trimmed, plowed, graded, planted, and fenced, its dusty bare ground grazed to the nub. It appeared that humans had been here, fixing Mother Nature. The other side was completely wild, nearly every plant blooming vigorously. The wholeness and new growth lifted my spirits. No wonder the gate sings! It wants to remind me that this is a portal to a very special place.

Whenever I pass through the song gate, heading out, the song seems sweet, like a welcoming to the solitude. Coming back, the song sounds sad and lonesome.

Black Mountain

On the 26th of October, 1985, old friends gathered for dinner in a high canyon formerly owned by grizzly bears. Rancho Mañana was having a party, and there was food, laughter, and song until late in the evening.

After all the children ran out of noise and everybody else went to sleep, three old buddies sat by a stone-ringed fire. Two were having birthdays. The full moon was rising, and lighting up the hillside like day. There was talk of the big fire that had swept through on July 3rd, burning the chaparral down to the root burls. For the first time in twenty years, a hiker could go places inaccessible before the fire.

A moonlight walk sounded like a good idea, so, without much forethought, we started up Oso Creek. Climbing over rocks with ease, we worked our way along, pushing each other to keep going higher. We hoped the coolness of the night might keep the rattlesnakes away, as up we went.

The path we'd chosen got steeper, and turned into an uneven rubble stairway. All the rocks were loose, and soon we had to separate to keep from knocking rocks down on each other. When the rocks did fall, it was a spectacular sight.

As the boulders bounced down the canyon, every time they hit, sparks would fly in the semidarkness. And every time they hit, they broke into many pieces, and the pieces sparked and broke, making spark showers all the way down the mountain. It was a good thing the brush had already burned!

After about two hours of climbing, we thought we might be halfway up, and decided to make for the top. There were stumps of burned brush everywhere, and this made the climbing easier. Many times we traveled sideways to get around steep places. Finally we made it to a ridgeline and followed it up.

The climb was easier once we were off the cliff face. No one had a watch with them, but the westering moon told us it was about 3 a.m. when we broke over the top of the of the Topa Topa bluffs.

What a sight! We could see the lights of the entire county, all the way from Santa Barbara to the Conejo Grade. The moonlight shimmering on the ocean was my favorite sight.

As we stood there huffing and puffing from the climb, someone asked, "Did anybody think to bring water?" I remember saying, based on all my trips up there, "Don't worry, there's always water up high."

As we wandered around, looking for a place to lie down and rest, we saw the moon being reflected off the top of a rock. A small pool of water appeared, left by some rain that had fallen a week before. After quenching our thirst, we made some sagebrush beds and slept till dawn.

As the light came, I looked at my friends and had a good laugh. They were black from head to toe from grabbing charcoal branches during our ascent, and so was I!

The trip back down took only two hours. It's amazing how fast you can descend when you're hungry.

What a birthday! Whenever Wayne, Marty, and I get together, our four-thousand-foot moonlight climb always comes up in the conversation. And I can honestly say that the three of us now know what it feels like to be black!

The Bungee Jumper

For many years, Hugh Estill and I made a third-weekend-in-May pilgrimage to the Calaveras County Fair. I had a frog suit left over from a Fourth of July float, and brought it with me every year to work the gate. We took turns being the frog welcoming people to the jump. Tom Weddle lived up there, and volunteered to help park cars; he was our "in."

One year it happened to be the first time that they offered bungee jumping as one of the attractions. We were taking a break inside the gate, and decided to go watch border collies work the sheep. There was a lot going on. Besides the jumping frogs and sheepdogs, there were ten thousand people to watch.

Hugh had an uncanny ability to pick out the most promisingly profound situations anywhere around, so when he said, "Watch this," he had my full attention. There in the field, beside the place where everything was going on, sat a boom truck with a very large ladder fully extended. Going up that fully extended ladder was the bungee operator, and following him up was a woman.

I hadn't (and still haven't) had much experience with bungee jumping, but I could tell at a glance that this woman had no future in this field. She didn't look like anyone who should be attempting flight, but I had to give her credit. She was fearless.

When they got to the launch area near the top, the man tied one cord on her, looked her over, and then tied a second one on for good measure. Then he put his hands up in the air, showing her how to launch herself properly. Suddenly frogs and dogs held no interest whatsoever for Hugh and me and the rest of the crowd. It was like witnessing the space shuttle; the whole place stopped to watch.

She leaned back with her arms straight up and peeled off that tower like nothing we ever saw. Down she came in a beautiful arc, and when she hit the ends of those rubber bands, her blouse just kept right on going. What a sight!

She bounced up and down a couple of times before she stopped. And then there she was, hanging upside down from the rubber bands, swaying in the breeze in her pink brassiere.

The ovation for her was long and generous, and we all felt good. She gave it up for us and we gave it up for her. Most everyone seemed to feel that this part of the entertainment had been well worth the price of admission.

She laughed when they let her down . . . what a gal! I felt she was someone worth knowing, but by the time I got over there she was lost in the crowd.

Frog Wranglers

The owner of a local oil company commissioned me to make something with frogs in it as a gift for his wife. It was a good reason for a little outdoor adventure. Lucky for me, I had at my beck and call two fine young boys willing to try almost anything if it sounded like fun. I told them that I was in urgent need of a frog to use as a model for my project. Would they come along and help me catch one?

Yes was the unanimous response of my small but enthusiastic crew, and yes was the response from their mother. We grabbed a flashlight and an old Coleman lantern. The only fishnet I could find had a frog-sized hole in it, but I took it anyway. The sun was going down as we loaded up my VW van with buckets and extra clothes.

A half hour later, we pulled into the upper Rose Valley Lake parking area and unloaded like a noisy little SWAT team. "Sh-h-h-h-h-h—be very quiet," I told my mighty crew.

Armed with bucket, flashlight, and holed net, we set off for our date with destiny. In the dark, we could already hear the frog-er-nacle choir singing wildly away in the cattails. We crested the hill and slunk down along the shoreline in search of our first victim. My fearless crew, having never caught wild frogs before, followed close behind me, no doubt wondering if they would survive the night.

I switched on the light and shone it down the beach. There, not more then ten feet away, sat a nice big bullfrog! I held the light steady, shining right in its eyes, and handing the net to the frog wranglers I said, "Catch that frog!"

The boys went out ahead of me, net held high, slipping and sliding in the dirt and mud. The net came down squarely over the beast, followed by much splashing and screaming.

"Did you catch it?"

"No, it got away," was the report from the crew. "It jumped out of the hole in the net."

"Okay," I said, "we need a change of strategy. Give me the net, and you take the flashlight."

The next frog was not far up the beach. "Shine the light on it," I directed, "and I'll see what I can do."

Swish went the net! After two quick jumps, the frog found the hole and got away.

The third frog was a large female. I slapped the net over her, picked her up before she could jump out, and tossed her onto the bank, about fifteen feet behind my surprised young crew. When she hit the ground, she knew exactly which way the water was (downhill), and here she came back, flying through the air in great jumps!

The boys had never faced a charging bullfrog before, and they did the first thing that came to mind—run! The only way to retreat was into the lake. One passed me on the right, the other on the left, and almost at the same instant I was struck soundly in the knee by a large flying frog, and we all ended up together—soaking wet in the lake!

"Now we know what to expect," I told my trusty crew." Let's go catch some frogs."

We worked our way around the whole lake that night, netting and pitching bullfrogs. The frog catchers got past their fear and landed about three. (The rest got away clean.) We turned two loose and brought one home in a bucket to study.

When we got home late that night, there was a loud scream from the boys' mother as we marched in the front door. We looked in the mirror and saw three happy, dark-brown frog wranglers, covered in mud, staring back at us.

P.S. Two days later, we took the frog back to the lake.

When Yesterday Met Tomorrow

It was late spring in Ojai, and Theresa had come down from Alaska to visit Hugh Estill, her aging father. Winter in the far north had been cold, dark, and long. She needed a little sunshine. Along with her came a new baby, just old enough to stand on two shaky legs.

My grandmother was in a rest home, and it was about time for a visit. I asked Theresa if she'd like to take a little ride over to meet my gram and then look at the wildflowers on the way back, and the answer was yes. We drove slowly over the hill to the next town. The backcountry was in full bloom.

We parked at the rest home and walked in. As we entered the building and began the search for my grandmother, Theresa's baby was laughing and making cute baby sounds. I noticed big smiles all around the normally grumpy old day room. Everyone had noticed the little baby.

People who hadn't felt like moving in years were scooting about, trying to get close. They followed us around, causing a wheelchair traffic jam. Theresa stopped to let everyone see the young child. The baby noticed all her new admirers and reached out to touch them, and they reached out to touch her. The whole rest home warmed with happiness. People filled the hallways as word spread of the baby in their midst. It was a baby shower in the rest home!

Theresa let anyone hold the young child who wanted to. It took over an hour for the place to settle down.

I found my grandmother asleep in her room. Theresa let the baby wake her up by touching her face with those tiny little hands. When I talked to my gram about it later, she said, "I thought I had died and woke up in Heaven!"

In a Rut

'Twas October in Cambria—deer season. I was up there to help my old friend Ed finish a wooden rocking horse he had started fifty years ago as a gift for one of his children. Life got in the way, time passed, and now he just wanted to get it done. I felt honored to be asked to help.

Ed was away when I finally had time to sneak off from my life, but I went anyway. I got the key for the shop from Mitch, who was keeping an eye on the house while Ed was gone.

I set up a table out in the yard under the pine trees, and brought out the rocking horse. It had been roughed out nicely, but still needed some refining. Carved of laminated mahogany, it was a soft blonde color.

I started carving with Swiss chisels, and was quietly tapping when I noticed a large buck deer chewing under a nearby tree. Suddenly there was a crash in the bushes as another big buck broke into the clearing where I was working. Head down, nose up, he was looking for love. The first buck jumped up, gave a big snort, and charged.

Now, this was not quite how I'd pictured my morning going, but through the years I have learned to just go with it. The boys shoved each other around for a while, with nobody seeming to win. Then they took a little break, lost interest, and wandered off.

I had been so busy getting set up that I hadn't noticed before, but there were deer everywhere: under every tree and near the deck, the porch, and the table. They matched the color of the pine needles so well that the only time I could see them was when they wiggled their ears. As I woke to my surroundings, I counted seventeen deer around me!

And just when I thought I couldn't be any more thrilled, a lovely doe with two yearling fawns came bounding into view. The doe saw me and walked slowly away, but the fawns froze when they saw the rocking horse. I don't think they even noticed me. They stood perfectly still for a moment, then moved ever so slowly toward the table. It was so quiet I could hear their little ankles crack. The carving had them in its spell.

Closer and closer they came, until they touched it with those soft wet noses. Then, as they stepped back, they saw me and the spell was broken. They bounded off to find their mother.

As I went back to carving, I felt like I, too, had been touched by the warm, wet nose of Mother Nature.

P.S. It's dangerous out in the woods during mating season, so I later learned that all the deer make a tradition of going to Ed's.

Who knew?

Once in a Blue Moon

The date was July 31, 2004. I was on my way back to Ojai, California, from Lemon, South Dakota, where I'd been digging up dinosaur bones for about a month. I ran out of daylight to drive in, and decided to stop and visit old friends in Templeton for the night.

Frank and Donna had four hundred acres of old-growth almond trees back in the rolling hills. Rick DeRamus was their ranch manager. When passing through, I liked to stop and hear what had been going on. One of the highlights of each visit was always a nice long walk, to get the blood circulating after driving for so long.

On this particular night, I got there late and decided the talk was more important; I could walk in the morning. Tall tales were told, and big stories exchanged, till after midnight. I said goodnight and went off to sleep.

When I woke up at about 4 a.m., the moon was going down in the west, making more than enough light for a pre-dawn walk. I left my shoes behind and climbed the dirt road through the almond trees. The setting moon cast long shadows across the land and my imagination came to life as I walked. A rabbit would take off almost under my feet, or a deer would break the dry grass as she bounded off. The owls were exchanging hoots; in the field, mice skittered about. It was like walking in a dream.

About an hour later, I returned to my van, opened the side door, and put on my shoes. After a few minutes of stargazing, I walked around, got in the van, and hit the starter. With the motor running, I reached down and turned on the headlights.

Out about twenty feet in front of my camper stood a very large male mountain lion, in his prime, as nice as you could ever ask to see. His big, round eyes reflected a bright yellow. I switched the lights off for a second, and he disappeared. His fur was exactly the same color as the dry grass and the dirt in the road. In an instant, he was invisible!

I switched the lights off and on several times, not believing what I was seeing. That lion stood there looking at me, so relaxed and gentle, like he wanted to play some more. I began to wonder how long he had followed me. I had just wandered the entire length and width of the ranch, barefoot, in shorts and no shirt, with only a walking stick. I don't remember ever looking back to see if anything was following me. I thought I was at the top of the food chain that morning! In any case, in the moonlight he was totally invisible, and I will never know.

As my van began moving toward my large, fuzzy new friend, he turned and padded off down the almond orchard road, leaving little puffs of dust hanging in the cool night air. Then he rounded the corner and started up the pavement on Almond Drive. I idled along, watching the way he moved. His tail was magnificent—the way it swung up and down in a slow circle as he loped along. He was so graceful. What an athlete—so confident and so powerful! His eyes flashed every time he turned to look at me.

The big cat knew the place well. After trotting up the road a piece, he ducked through a hole in the fence that deer had made, and simply disappeared. That's about when the fear caught up with me. My knees felt weak, and my whole body did a little shimmy. I drove off down the road, thinking about what a big difference there is between having breakfast and being breakfast.

Now I can say I've taken a walk with a mountain lion, once in a blue moon.

Ain't it great to be alive?

The Fairy Queen

I like to call it the madness of dawn. Long before sunrise you can hear the sound of trowels, shovels, and plastic buckets bumping around in the darkness, of fearless artisans of the sand drinking coffee, devouring donuts, and arguing about what to make. The gulls are confused by all the noise.

The people who work alone are quietly planning where to begin. As the light comes, digging starts in earnest. Huge piles of sand are stacked, packed, wetted down, and discussed as to best visual impact.

It's the Fourth of July in the Central California coastal city of Cayucos. Every year, the town shuts down to entertain itself. Church groups, old hippies, computer nerds, graffiti felons, Central Valley farmers, and children and their families all get together to make things out of sand.

The contest rules are simple:

1. Show up at dawn.
2. Don't sign up—just start.
3. South of the pier is for kids, north of it for everyone else.
4. Make anything you want.
5. Have a great time!
6. At nine o'clock they come around with the ribbons and trophies.
7. The parade starts at ten.

I've been contributing piles of shaped sand there for twenty years now. One year there was an antique auto show added to the roster, and that gave me an idea: I'd make an old-fashioned car out of sand.

As I stood near my favorite spot to dig, I noticed that the tide was headed way out. It would be a long walk to get water. Not far up the beach, a creek came out to a small lagoon. It doesn't matter what kind of water you use on sand to hold it together, so I set up next to the lagoon and started digging.

The tide just kept going out, farther and farther. People down the beach were walking a hundred yards to get a bucket of seawater. I told one young boy that the reason the ocean was so low was because people were taking too much water out, and I think he believed me.

As the sun came up, all the piles of sand began to wondrously turn into things. Harmony seemed to envelop the beach as the art became more focused. I was feeling pretty good about my project. I rounded the fenders, dug out the interior, and put eyes in the headlights. Then I set up the wood stick windshield frame and planted the steering wheel in the sand dashboard. Next came the tuck 'n' roll seats and the gearshift.

I was working on the spare tire on the back when I noticed some trouble heading my way. Far down the beach, someone had gotten sidetracked talking to old friends. The three-year-old girl they were not watching had seen my car and was heading for it like a torpedo. My heart sank . . . there's a certain look on a kid's face when they see something they like, and she had it. As I stood there watching, I thought fate might intervene, but when she got closer I realized this would be my lesson, not hers.

It was a joy to see someone so unhindered by prior experience. In her mind, this car had been built just for her. Who was I to tell her it wasn't? I stepped back out of the way and braced for impact.

She was so cute. She stopped for a moment to take it all in. Then, in one inspired, fluid motion, she stepped up on the running board and climbed in. She sat down on those beautiful tuck 'n' roll seats and grabbed the steering wheel. Suddenly she was magically transformed into a fairy queen! Off she went, making happy little noises, turning the steering wheel back and forth and singing.

I, too, was transformed. I went from grumpy old sand sculptor to a little boy who loved playing in the sand. As I watched her dream, I remembered my own dreams. Everyone around me did the same . . . we all remembered.

Suddenly, reality struck. The woman whose child had gotten away—the mom—came running up, and in an instant the spell was broken. She pulled the fairy queen out of the dream and gave her a little shake before setting her back down on the sand. The beautiful little girl began to cry. The mother turned to me and said, "I'm so sorry about this!"

I looked at my young friend and said, "I'll fix it; it's just sand." But the damage had already been done.

The woman carried the weeping child away, and I went back to sculpting. In ten minutes you couldn't tell the fairy queen had ever paid a visit, except for the tears and tiny footprints in my heart.

Not long after, the judges came by and gave me a plastic trophy, and everyone clapped. But still I felt sad.

The Trespass

Somewhere in the great, rolling badlands of eastern Nevada, I came upon a fence in the middle of nowhere. I stood for a long time in front of its "No Trespassing" sign, trying to decide whom it was posted there for.

It couldn't have been for me. I'm a nice guy. I don't steal things. I'm great company—quiet and easygoing. I love to explore lonely places. The sign must have been meant for someone else.

I got down on my hands and knees and crawled under the fence. I was barefoot, wearing shorts and no shirt, and carrying a stick with a carved frog on the top.

I could see for five miles in every direction, and there was not a ranch house in sight, not a soul around. Just this fence with a sign . . . for someone else. I headed in to the great unknown.

In the distance I could see a gulch lined with cottonwoods, and that's where I headed. Maybe I'd find a creek with some water.

The sagebrush was waist-high, and filled with game trails. I moved easily along, looking at animal tracks in the soft soil. I remember daydreaming and listening to the birds.

About a quarter mile from the fence, I first heard something big, running. The sound was far away, but it seemed to be getting closer. I could hear something crashing through the brush, and then heavy breathing. Whatever was coming was really moving.

I began to look around for a tree or a pile of rocks to get up on so I could see, but there was nothing but sagebrush. The river was still a long way off. I was running down the trail now, and looking over my shoulder. Finally I saw the beast, coming after me at full speed.

It was a teenage black bull, weighing probably a thousand pounds, with his head down and his sharp horns pointed forward. He appeared to be a wild Spanish bull of the kind that still run in Pamplona. And he was gaining on me.

Then I saw it—my salvation. Sticking up about four feet from the ground, just above the sagebrush, was the cut-off stump of a telephone pole about a foot thick. I don't know how I got up on it, but there I was on top of it just as the bull caught up with me. I stood there like a cornered bobcat while the bull put on his brakes and tried to figure out what to do next. I remember thinking, Thank the spirits it wasn't a bear!

The bull horned my cedar pole several times, but when he put his head down to charge, his horns struck lower than where my bare feet were perched. His force did shake the pole, but luckily for me I had my frog stick to help keep my balance.

He ran around me several times, snorting and stomping, and then just stood back and watched. It was looking to be a long, hot day.

The bull wandered around for a while, coming back to check on me two or three times. It's hard to look casual while balancing on the stump of a telephone pole, but I did my best to not antagonize him. Then he turned away from me with his ears up. I guess he heard something else, because he took off at a dead run again.

I listened to his hoofbeats going away for a minute that seemed like an hour, then I climbed down and headed for the fence. When I got back safely on the other side of it, I decided maybe that "No Trespassing" sign *did* mean me.